# Keeping Fit

Level 7 – Turquoise

# Helpful Hints for Reading at Home

The graphemes (written letters) and phonemes (units of sound) used throughout this series are aligned with Letters and Sounds. This offers a consistent approach to learning whether reading at home or in the classroom.

**HERE IS A LIST OF PHONEMES FOR THIS PHASE OF LEARNING. AN EXAMPLE OF THE PRONUNCIATION CAN BE FOUND IN BRACKETS.**

| Phase 5 | | | |
|---|---|---|---|
| ay (day) | ou (out) | ie (tie) | ea (eat) |
| oy (boy) | ir (girl) | ue (blue) | aw (saw) |
| wh (when) | ph (photo) | ew (new) | oe (toe) |
| au (Paul) | a_e (make) | e_e (these) | i_e (like) |
| o_e (home) | u_e (rule, cube) | | |

| Phase 5 Alternative Pronunciations of Graphemes | | | |
|---|---|---|---|
| a (hat, what) | e (bed, she) | i (fin, find) | o (hot, so, other) |
| u (but, unit) | c (cat, cent) | g (got, giant) | ow (cow, blow) |
| ie (tied, field) | ea (eat, bread) | er (farmer, herb) | ch (chin, school, chef) |
| y (yes, by, very) | ou (out, shoulder, could, you) | | |

**HERE ARE SOME WORDS WHICH YOUR CHILD MAY FIND TRICKY.**

| Phase 5 Tricky Words | | | |
|---|---|---|---|
| oh | their | people | Mr |
| Mrs | looked | called | asked |
| could | | | |

## TOP TIPS FOR HELPING YOUR CHILD TO READ:

- Allow children time to break down unfamiliar words into units of sound and then encourage children to string these sounds together to create the word.

- Encourage your child to point out any focus phonics when they are used.

- Read through the book more than once to grow confidence.

- Ask simple questions about the text to assess understanding.

- Encourage children to use illustrations as prompts.

This book focuses on the alternative pronunciation of the grapheme /c/ and is a Turquoise level 7 book band.

Can you sort these words into two groups?
One group has c as in **cat**.
One group has c as in **face**.

doctor

decide

cone

fact

count

pencil

place

cent

It is important to stay fit. We can stay fit with sports and exercise. Do you have a sport that you like to do?

This girl is running.

First, we must make sure that we eat and drink specific things. Milk has a lot of calcium in it. Calcium helps our bones stay strong.

Running is a good way to stay fit. We can run with other people. We can run in a race. Racing is exciting!

Step up to the line, get set... go!

Are you quick at running? If you have the pace to win a race, you could run against people in a marathon. A marathon is a long race.

What was the most recent sport you saw? Did you see football? In football, you need skill and a slice of luck to win. Football keeps us fit.

There is a lot of running in football. We run into space for a player to pass the ball. We face the keeper and shoot to win.

There are a lot of sports to do. Ice hockey is different to a lot of sports. We play ice hockey on an ice rink, with ice skates on our feet.

It is normal to slip. It can hurt, so you must brace if you fall on the ice! If you fall twice, do not let it stop you having a go!

Can you bend a lot? If you can, you could be an acrobat. Acrobats must keep fit to perform. You can see acrobats at the circus.

The circus is ace. Acrobats can flip and spin in a loop. You need to do specific training to be in the circus.

This acrobat is upside down!

Do not say no the next time you get asked to exercise. It is good for you. Go and see what sports you can do to keep fit.

You might win a race with people in class. You might turn into a circus acrobat. You might win a football match. These are good ways to keep fit!

©2022 **BookLife Publishing Ltd.**
King's Lynn, Norfolk, PE30 4LS, UK

ISBN 978-1-80155-811-2

All rights reserved. Printed in Poland.
A catalogue record for this book is available
from the British Library.

**Keeping Fit**
Written by William Anthony
Designed by Drue Rintoul

# An Introduction to BookLife Readers...

Our Readers have been specifically created in line with the London Institute of Education's approach to book banding and are phonetically decodable and ordered to support each phase of the Letters and Sounds document.

Each book has been created to provide the best possible reading and learning experience. Our aim is to share our love of books with children, providing both emerging readers and prolific page-turners with beautiful books that are guaranteed to provoke interest and learning, regardless of ability.

**BOOK BAND GRADED** using the Institute of Education's approach to levelling.

**PHONETICALLY DECODABLE** supporting each phase of Letters and Sounds.

**EXERCISES AND QUESTIONS** to offer reinforcement and to ascertain comprehension.

**CLEAR DESIGN** to inspire and provoke engagement, providing the reader with clear visual representations of each non-fiction topic.

**AUTHOR INSIGHT:**
**WILLIAM ANTHONY**

William Anthony's involvement with children's education is quite extensive. He has written over 60 titles with BookLife Publishing so far, across a wide range of subjects. William graduated from Cardiff University with a 1st Class BA (Hons) in Journalism, Media and Culture, creating an app and a TV series, among other things, during his time there.

William Anthony has also produced work for the Prince's Trust, a charity created by HRH The Prince of Wales, that helps young people with their professional future. He has created animated videos for a children's education company that works closely with the charity.

**PHASE 5**
/c/

This book focuses on the alternative pronunciation of the grapheme /c/ and is a turquoise level 7 book band.

**Image Credits** Images are courtesy of Shutterstock.com. With thanks to Getty Images, Thinkstock Photo and iStockphoto. Cover – VaLiza, zhu difeng, MaryDesy. p4–5 – Niyazz, Angelo Giampiccolo. p6–7 – Ana Flasker, cktravels.com. p8–9 – Wirestock Creators, Dirk M. de Boer, COULANGES. p10–11 – BlueOrange Studio, Wasim Khuzam. p12–13 – gorillaimages, FooTToo. p14–15 – Odua Images, Monkey Business Images.